To

_____

From

_____

BroadStreet Publishing
Racine, WI 53403
Broadstreetpublishing.com

BIBLE PROMISES *for You*

© 2014 by BroadStreet Publishing Group, LLC.

ISBN 978-1-4245-5097-5

Compiled by Michelle Winger | literallyprecise.com
Designed by Chris Garborg | garborgdesign.com

Printed in China

BIBLE PROMISES
for You

BroadStreet
PUBLISHING

Everything you need to get through each day can be found in the promises of God's Word. *Bible Promises for You* is a topically organized collection of Scripture that is designed to help you recognize who you are, and who you can be, when you embrace the truth of His Word. Each theme declares a promise you can claim over your life and Bible verses to help you grab hold of that promise.

Find the inspiration and encouragement you need in God's Word. His promises are for you every day!

CONTENTS

I am Able

We are not saying that we can do this work ourselves.
It is God who makes us able to do all that we do.

2 Corinthians 3:5 ncv

Take a new grip with your tired hands and strengthen
your weak knees. Mark out a straight path for your feet
so that those who are weak and lame will not fall
but become strong.

Hebrews 12:12-13 nlt

"My grace is sufficient for you, for my power is made
perfect in weakness." Therefore I will boast all the
more gladly of my weaknesses, so that the power of
Christ may rest upon me.

2 Corinthians 12:9 esv

We can rejoice, too, when we run into problems and trials, for we know that they help us develop endurance. And endurance develops strength of character, and character strengthens our confident hope of salvation. And this hope will not lead to disappointment. For we know how dearly God loves us, because he has given us the Holy Spirit to fill our hearts with his love.

ROMANS 5:3–5 NLT

After you have suffered for a little while, the God of all grace, who called you to His eternal glory in Christ, will Himself perfect, confirm, strengthen and establish you.

1 PETER 5:10 NASB

I am Accepted

The Father gives me the people who are mine. Every one
of them will come to me, and I will always accept them.

JOHN 6:37 NCV

Before he made the world, God chose us to be his very
own through what Christ would do for us; he decided
then to make us holy in his eyes, without a single fault—
we who stand before him covered with his love.

EPHESIANS 1:4 TLB

If God is for us, who can be against us?

ROMANS 8:31 ESV

Here I am! I stand at the door and knock. If anyone hears
my voice and opens the door, I will come in and eat with
that person, and they with me.

Revelation 3:20 NIV

I've redeemed you.

I've called your name. You're mine.

When you're in over your head, I'll be there with you.

When you're in rough waters, you will not go down.

When you're between a rock and a hard place,

it won't be a dead end—

Because I am God, your personal God,

The Holy of Israel, your Savior.

I paid a huge price for you...!

That's how much you mean to me!

That's how much I love you!

Isaiah 43:1–4 MSG

I am Adopted

You did not receive a spirit of slavery to fall back into fear, but you have received a spirit of adoption. When we cry, "Abba! Father!" it is that very Spirit bearing witness with our spirit that we are children of God.

ROMANS 8:15–16 NRSV

The LORD will not abandon His people on account of His great name, because the LORD has been pleased to make you a people for Himself.

1 SAMUEL 12:22 NASB

I will not abandon you as orphans—I will come to you.

JOHN 14:18 NLT

A father of the fatherless and a judge for the widows,

Is God in His holy habitation.

God makes a home for the lonely;

He leads out the prisoners into prosperity.

PSALM 68:5-6 NASB

But when the right time came, God sent his Son, born of a woman, subject to the law. God sent him to buy freedom for us who were slaves to the law, so that he could adopt us as his very own children.

GALATIANS 4:4-5 NLT

I will bring the blind by a way they did not know;

I will lead them in paths they have not known.

I will make darkness light before them,

And crooked places straight.

These things will I do for them,

And not forsake them.

ISAIAH 42:16 NKJV

I am Alive

Dear friend, listen well to my words;

tune your ears to my voice.

Keep my message in plain view at all times.

Concentrate! Learn it by heart!

Those who discover these words live,

really live; body and soul....

Keep vigilant watch over your heart;

that's where life starts.

PROVERBS 4:20–23 MSG

I am the resurrection and the life. He who believes in Me,

though he may die, he shall live.

JOHN 11:25 NKJV

Sin...doesn't, have a chance in competition with the aggressive forgiveness we call *grace*. When it's sin versus grace, grace wins hands down. All sin can do is threaten us with death.... Grace...invites us into life—a life that goes on and on and on, world without end.

Romans 5:20–21 msg

I am the Light of the world; he who follows Me will not walk in the darkness, but will have the Light of life.

John 8:12 nasb

We're not giving up. How could we! Even though on the outside it often looks like things are falling apart on us, on the inside, where God is making new life, not a day goes by without his unfolding grace.

2 Corinthians 4:16 msg

I am Assured

Your promises have been thoroughly tested,
and your servant loves them.
…My eyes stay open through the watches of the night,
that I may meditate on your promises.

PSALM 119:140, 148 NIV

He has granted to us his precious and very great promises,
so that through them you may become partakers of the
divine nature, having escaped from the corruption that is
in the world.

2 PETER 1:3-4 ESV

To him who is able to do immeasurably more than all
we ask or imagine, according to his power that is at work
within us, to him be glory…for ever and ever! Amen.

EPHESIANS 3:20–21 NIV

All of God's promises have been fulfilled in Christ
with a resounding "Yes!"

2 Corinthians 1:20 nlt

These things I have written to you who believe in the
name of the Son of God, that you may know that you
have eternal life, and that you may continue to believe in
the name of the Son of God.

1 John 5:13 nkjv

Jesus Christ is the same yesterday and today and forever.

Hebrews 13:8 nasb

The Lord always keeps his promises;
he is gracious in all he does.

Psalm 145:13 nlt

I am Authentic

If you're content to simply be yourself,
your life will count for plenty.

MATTHEW 23:12 MSG

It's who you are and the way you live that count before
God. Your worship must engage your spirit in the pursuit
of truth. That's the kind of people the Father is out
looking for: those who are simply and honestly *themselves*
before him in their worship. God is sheer being itself—
Spirit. Those who worship him must do it out of their
very being, their spirits, their true selves, in adoration.

JOHN 4:23–24 MSG

Take your everyday, ordinary life—your sleeping, eating, going-to-work, and walking-around life—and place it before God as an offering. Embracing what God does for you is the best thing you can do for him. Don't become so well-adjusted to your culture that you fit into it without even thinking. Instead, fix your attention on God. You'll be changed from the inside out. Readily recognize what he wants from you, and quickly respond to it. Unlike the culture around you, always dragging you down to its level of immaturity, God brings the best out of you, develops well-formed maturity in you.

ROMANS 12:1–2 MSG

I am Beautiful

I will praise You,
for I am fearfully and wonderfully made;
Marvelous are Your works,
And that my soul knows very well.

PSALM 139:14 NKJV

Don't be concerned about the outward beauty of fancy
hairstyles, expensive jewelry, or beautiful clothes. You
should clothe yourselves instead with the beauty that
comes from within, the unfading beauty of a gentle and
quiet spirit, which is so precious to God.

1 PETER 3:3–4 NLT

The Lord doesn't see things the way you see them.
People judge by outward appearance,
but the Lord looks at the heart.

1 Samuel 16:7 nlt

Has anyone by fussing in front of the mirror ever gotten
taller by so much as an inch? All this time and money
wasted on fashion—do you think it makes that much
difference? Instead of looking at the fashions, walk out
into the fields and look at the wildflowers. They never
primp or shop, but have you ever seen color and design
quite like it? The ten best-dressed men and women in the
country look shabby alongside them.

Matthew 6:27–29 msg

He has made everything beautiful in its time.

Ecclesiastes 3:11 niv

I am Befriended

The LORD is near to all who call on him,
to all who call on him in truth.

PSALM 145:18 NIV

Here I am! I stand at the door and knock. If anyone hears
my voice and opens the door, I will come in and eat with
that person, and they with me.

REVELATION 3:20 NIV

Turn to me and have mercy,
for I am alone and in deep distress.

PSALM 25:16 NLT

The amazing grace of the Master, Jesus Christ, the
extravagant love of God, the intimate friendship of the

Holy Spirit, be with all of you.

2 Corinthians 13:14 msg

The right word at the right time
is like a custom-made piece of jewelry,
And a wise friend's timely reprimand
is like a gold ring slipped on your finger.
Reliable friends who do what they say
are like cool drinks in sweltering heat—refreshing!

Proverbs 25:12–13 msg

By this we know that we abide in Him and He in us,
because He has given us of His Spirit.

1 John 4:13 nasb

A friend loves at all times.

Proverbs 17:17 nkjv

Behold, I am with you always, to the end of the age.

Matthew 28:20 esv

I am Blessed

You prepare a feast for me
in the presence of my enemies.
You honor me by anointing my head with oil.
My cup overflows with blessings.

PSALM 23:5 NLT

Blessed be the God and Father of our Lord Jesus Christ,
who has blessed us in Christ with every spiritual blessing
in the heavenly places, even as he chose us in him before
the foundation of the world, that we should be holy and
blameless before him.

EPHESIANS 1:3–4 ESV

How blessed all those in whom you live,
whose lives become roads you travel;
They wind through lonesome valleys, come upon brooks,
discover cool springs and pools brimming with rain!

Psalm 84:5–6 msg

From his abundance we have all received one gracious
blessing after another.

John 1:16 nlt

For the Lord God is our sun and our shield.
He gives us grace and glory.
The Lord will withhold no good thing
from those who do what is right.

Psalm 84:11 nlt

The Lord bless you, and keep you;
The Lord make His face shine on you,
And be gracious to you;
The Lord lift up His countenance on you,
And give you peace.

Numbers 6:24–26 nasb

I am Calm

Be still in the presence of the Lord,

and wait patiently for him to act.

Don't worry about evil people who prosper

or fret about their wicked schemes.

Stop being angry!

Turn from your rage!

Do not lose your temper—

it only leads to harm.

PSALM 37:7-8 NLT

Let not your heart be troubled.

You are trusting God, now trust in me.

JOHN 14:1 TLB

Cast all your anxiety on him because he cares for you.

1 PETER 5:7 NIV

Be still, and know that I am God.

I will be exalted among the nations,

I will be exalted in the earth!

PSALM 46:10 ESV

Do not be anxious about anything, but in every situation,

by prayer and petition, with thanksgiving, present

your requests to God.

PHILIPPIANS 4:6 NIV

In my trouble I cried to the LORD,

And He answered me.

PSALM 120:1 NASB

I want you woven into a tapestry of love, in touch with

everything there is to know of God. Then you will have

minds confident and at rest, focused on Christ,

God's great mystery.

COLOSSIANS 2:2 MSG

Trusting me, you will be unshakable and assured, deeply at

peace. In this godless world you will continue to experience

difficulties. But take heart! I've conquered the world.

JOHN 16:33 MSG

I am Cherished

The LORD directs the steps of the godly.
He delights in every detail of their lives.
Though they stumble, they will never fall,
for the LORD holds them by the hand.

PSALM 37:23–24 NLT

I am sure that neither death nor life, nor angels nor rulers,
nor things present nor things to come, nor powers, nor height
nor depth, nor anything else in all creation, will be able to
separate us from the love of God in Christ Jesus our Lord.

ROMANS 8:38–39 ESV

He tends his flock like a shepherd:

He gathers the lambs in his arms

and carries them close to his heart;

he gently leads those that have young.

Isaiah 40:11 niv

Blessed be the Lord,

Because He has heard the voice of my supplication.

The Lord is my strength and my shield;

My heart trusts in Him, and I am helped;

Therefore my heart exults,

And with my song I shall thank Him.

Psalm 28:6-7 nasb

You're blessed when you feel you've lost what is
most dear to you. Only then can you be embraced
by the One most dear to you.

Matthew 5:4 msg

I am Chosen

How blessed is God!... Long before he laid down earth's
foundations, he had us in mind, had settled on us as the
focus of his love, to be made whole and holy by his love.
Long, long ago he decided to adopt us into his family
through Jesus Christ. (What pleasure he took in planning
this!) He wanted us to enter into the celebration of his
lavish gift-giving by the hand of his beloved Son.

EPHESIANS 1:3–6 MSG

We know that all things work together for good
to those who love God, to those who are the called
according to His purpose.

ROMANS 8:28 NKJV

Confirm God's invitation to you, his choice of you.
Don't put it off; do it now. Do this, and you'll have
your life on a firm footing.

2 PETER 1:10–11 MSG

There is a time for everything,
and everything on earth has its special season.

ECCLESIASTES 3:1 NCV

No eye has seen, no ear has heard,
and no mind has imagined
what God has prepared
for those who love him.

1 CORINTHIANS 2:9 NLT

You are a chosen people, a royal priesthood, a holy nation,
God's special possession, that you may declare the praises of
him who called you out of darkness into his wonderful light.

1 PETER 2:9 NIV

I am Comforted

To all who mourn...he will give: beauty for ashes;
joy instead of mourning; praise instead of heaviness.
For God has planted them like strong and
graceful oaks for his own glory.

ISAIAH 61:3 TLB

May your unfailing love be my comfort,
according to your promise to your servant.

PSALM 119:76 NIV

May our Lord Jesus Christ himself and God our Father,
who loved us and by his grace gave us eternal comfort and
a wonderful hope, comfort you and strengthen you.

2 THESSALONIANS 2:16–17 NLT

Unless the LORD had helped me,

I would soon have settled in the silence of the grave.

I cried out, "I am slipping!"

but your unfailing love, O LORD, supported me.

When doubts filled my mind,

your comfort gave me renewed hope and cheer.

PSALM 94:17–19 NLT

Praise be to the God and Father of our Lord Jesus Christ,

the Father of compassion and the God of all comfort.

2 CORINTHIANS 1:3 NIV

God's dwelling place is now among the people, and he will

dwell with them…. "He will wipe every tear from their

eyes. There will be no more death" or mourning or crying

or pain, for the old order of things has passed away.

REVELATION 21:3–4 NIV

I am Confident

Be my rock of refuge,

to which I can always go;

give the command to save me,

for you are my rock and my fortress....

You have been my hope, Sovereign Lord,

my confidence since my youth.

Psalm 71:3, 5 niv

This is the confidence that we have toward him, that if we
ask anything according to his will he hears us. And if we
know that he hears us in whatever we ask, we know that
we have the requests that we have asked of him.

1 John 5:14–15 esv

Let us then approach God's throne of grace with confidence, so that we may receive mercy and find grace to help us in our time of need.

HEBREWS 4:16 NIV

We can confidently say, "The Lord is my helper; I will not fear; what can man do to me?"

HEBREWS 13:6 ESV

I am confident of this very thing, that He who began a good work in you will perfect it until the day of Christ Jesus.

PHILIPPIANS 1:6 NASB

But if you remain in me and my words remain in you, you may ask for anything you want, and it will be granted!

JOHN 15:7 NLT

I can do everything through Christ, who gives me strength.

PHILIPPIANS 4:13 NLT

I am Content

Oh, how sweet the light of day,
and how wonderful to live in the sunshine!
Even if you live a long time,
don't take a single day for granted.
Take delight in each light-filled hour.

ECCLESIASTES 11:7–8 MSG

I know what it is to be in need, and I know what it is to
have plenty. I have learned the secret of being content
in any and every situation, whether well fed or hungry,
whether living in plenty or in want. I can do all this
through him who gives me strength.

PHILIPPIANS 4:12-13 NIV

If God cares so wonderfully for wildflowers that are here today and thrown into the fire tomorrow, he will certainly care for you. Why do you have so little faith? So don't worry about these things, saying, "What will we eat? What will we drink? What will we wear?" These things dominate the thoughts of unbelievers, but your heavenly Father already knows all your needs. Seek the Kingdom of God above all else, and live righteously, and he will give you everything you need.

MATTHEW 6:30-33 NLT

You're blessed when you're content with just who you are— no more, no less. That's the moment you find yourselves proud owners of everything that can't be bought.

MATTHEW 5:5 MSG

I am Courageous

Love the LORD, all you godly ones!
For the LORD protects those who are loyal to him,
but he harshly punishes the arrogant.
So be strong and courageous,
all you who put your hope in the LORD!

PSALM 31:23–24 NLT

May he give you the power to accomplish all the good
things your faith prompts you to do.

2 THESSALONIANS 1:11 NLT

Be strong and courageous. Do not be frightened,
and do not be dismayed, for the LORD your God
is with you wherever you go.

JOSHUA 1:9 ESV

Even though I walk through the valley of the shadow of death,
I fear no evil, for You are with me;
Your rod and Your staff, they comfort me.

Psalm 23:4 nasb

I eagerly expect and hope that I will in no way be
ashamed, but will have sufficient courage so that
now as always Christ will be exalted in my body,
whether by life or by death.

Philippians 1:20 niv

When I am afraid, I put my trust in you.
In God, whose word I praise—
in God I trust and am not afraid.

Psalm 56:3–4 niv

Be on guard. Stand firm in the faith. Be courageous.
Be strong. And do everything with love.

1 Corinthians 16:13–14 nlt

I am Creative

Having then gifts differing according to the grace that is given to us, let us use them.

ROMANS 12:6 NKJV

The heavens are telling of the glory of God;
And their expanse is declaring the work of His hands.

PSALM 19:1 NASB

O LORD, what a variety of things you have made!
In wisdom you have made them all.
The earth is full of your creatures.

PSALM 104:24 NLT

Be sure to use the abilities God has given you.

1 TIMOTHY 4:14 TLB

The LORD is the one who shaped the mountains,
stirs up the winds, and reveals his thoughts to mankind.
He turns the light of dawn into darkness
and treads on the heights of the earth.
The LORD God of Heaven's Armies is his name!

AMOS 4:13 NLT

He has filled him with divine spirit, with skill, intelligence,
and knowledge in every kind of craft.

EXODUS 35:31 NRSV

Let the beauty of the LORD our God be upon us,
And establish the work of our hands for us.

PSALM 90:17 NKJV

A man's gift makes room for him
And brings him before great men.

PROVERBS 18:16 NASB

Do you see people skilled in their work?
They will work for kings, not for ordinary people.

PROVERBS 22:29 NCV

I am Defended

Beloved, do not avenge yourselves, but rather give place to wrath; for it is written, "Vengeance is Mine, I will repay," says the Lord.

Romans 12:19 nkjv

He will not break the bruised reed, nor quench the dimly burning flame. He will encourage the fainthearted, those tempted to despair. He will see full justice given to all who have been wronged.

Isaiah 42:3 tlb

The Lord secures justice for the poor and upholds the cause of the needy.

Psalm 140:12 niv

He will not judge by appearance, false evidence,
or hearsay, but will defend the poor and the exploited.
He will rule against the wicked who oppress them. For he
will be clothed with fairness and with truth.

ISAIAH 11:3–5 TLB

He did not retaliate when he was insulted,
nor threaten revenge when he suffered.
He left his case in the hands of God,
who always judges fairly.

1 PETER 2:23 NLT

LORD, you know the hopes of the helpless.
Surely you will hear their cries and comfort them.
You will bring justice to the orphans and the oppressed,
so mere people can no longer terrify them.

PSALM 10:17–18 NLT

Righteousness and justice
are the foundation of Your throne.

PSALM 89:14 NKJV

I am Delivered

I waited patiently for the LORD;

he turned to me and heard my cry.

He lifted me out of the slimy pit,

out of the mud and mire;

he set my feet on a rock

and gave me a firm place to stand.

He put a new song in my mouth,

a hymn of praise to our God.

Many will see and fear the LORD;

and put their trust in him.

PSALM 40:1–3 NIV

The LORD hears his people when they call to him for help.

He rescues them from all their troubles.

PSALM 34:17 NLT

Humble yourselves in the sight of the Lord,

and He will lift you up.

JAMES 4:10 NKJV

The righteous person faces many troubles,

but the LORD comes to the rescue each time.

PSALM 34:19 NLT

My prayer is to you, O LORD.

At an acceptable time, O God,

in the abundance of your steadfast love answer me in your

saving faithfulness.

Deliver me

from sinking in the mire;

let me be delivered from my enemies

and from the deep waters.

Answer me, O LORD , for your steadfast love is good;

according to your abundant mercy, turn to me.

PSALM 69:13-14, 16 ESV

I am Desired

I am my beloved's,
And his desire is toward me.

SONG OF SOLOMON 7:10 NKJV

It's in Christ that we find out who we are and what we
are living for. Long before we first heard of Christ and got
our hopes up, he had his eye on us, had designs on us for
glorious living, part of the overall purpose he is working
out in everything and everyone.

EPHESIANS 1:11–12 MSG

You make known to me the path of life;
you will fill me with joy in your presence,
with eternal pleasures at your right hand.

PSALM 16:11 NIV

The LORD your God is living among you.

He is a mighty savior.

He will take delight in you with gladness.

With his love, he will calm all your fears.

He will rejoice over you with joyful songs.

ZEPHANIAH 3:17 NLT

My God is changeless in his love for me,

and he will come and help me.

PSALM 59:10 TLB

My beloved speaks and says to me:

"Arise, my love, my beautiful one,

and come away,

for behold, the winter is past;

the rain is over and gone.

The flowers appear on the earth,

the time of singing has come."

SONG OF SOLOMON 2:10-12 ESV

I am Devoted

With all my heart I have sought You;

Do not let me wander from Your commandments.

Your word I have treasured in my heart,

That I may not sin against You.

…Teach me, O LORD, the way of Your statutes,

And I shall observe it to the end.

PSALM 119:10–11, 33 NASB

Seek first the kingdom of God and His righteousness, and

all these things shall be added to you.

MATTHEW 6:33 NKJV

Commit everything you do to the LORD.

Trust him, and he will help you.

PSALM 37:5 NLT

Stand firm. Let nothing move you. Always give yourselves
fully to the work of the Lord, because you know that your
labor in the Lord is not in vain.

1 Corinthians 15:58 niv

Commit your work to the Lord,
and your plans will be established.

Proverbs 16:3 esv

May God himself, the God of peace, sanctify you through
and through. May your whole spirit, soul and body be
kept blameless at the coming of our Lord Jesus Christ.
The one who calls you is faithful, and he will do it.

1 Thessalonians 5:23–24 niv

If any of you wants to be my follower, you must turn from
your selfish ways, take up your cross daily, and follow me.

Luke 9:23 nlt

I am Diligent

The plans of the diligent lead to profit
as surely as haste leads to poverty.

PROVERBS 21:5 NIV

To enjoy your work and to accept your lot in life—
that is indeed a gift from God. The person who does that
will not need to look back with sorrow on his past,
for God gives him joy.

ECCLESIASTES 5:20 TLB

In all the work you are doing, work the best you can.
Work as if you were doing it for the Lord, not for people.

COLOSSIANS 3:23 NCV

Be diligent in these matters; give yourself wholly to them,
so that everyone may see your progress.

1 TIMOTHY 4:15 NIV

Wise words bring many benefits,
and hard work brings rewards.

PROVERBS 12:14 NLT

Finish the work, so that your eager willingness to do it
may be matched by your completion of it,
according to your means.

2 CORINTHIANS 8:11 NIV

Pay careful attention to your own work,
for then you will get the satisfaction of a job well done,
and you won't need to compare yourself to anyone else.
For we are each responsible for our own conduct.

GALATIANS 6:4–5 NLT

I am Emboldened

We are pressed on every side by troubles, but we are not crushed. We are perplexed, but not driven to despair. We are hunted down, but never abandoned by God. We get knocked down, but we are not destroyed.

2 CORINTHIANS 4:8–9 NLT

If you're serious about living this new resurrection life with Christ, *act* like it. Pursue the things over which Christ presides. Don't shuffle along, eyes to the ground, absorbed with the things right in front of you. Look up, and be alert to what is going on around Christ—that's where the action is. See things from *his* perspective.

COLOSSIANS 3:1–2 MSG

Let us therefore come boldly to the throne of grace,

that we may obtain mercy and find grace

to help in time of need.

HEBREWS 4:16 NKJV

In all this you greatly rejoice, though now for a little while

you may have had to suffer grief in all kinds of trials.

These have come so that the proven genuineness of your

faith—of greater worth than gold, which perishes even

though refined by fire—may result in praise, glory and

honor when Jesus Christ is revealed.

1 PETER 1:6–7 NIV

I am Encouraged

Though an army besiege me,

my heart will not fear;

though war break out against me,

even then I will be confident.

One thing I ask from the Lord,

this only do I seek:

that I may dwell in the house of the Lord

all the days of my life,

to gaze on the beauty of the Lord

and to seek him in his temple.

For in the day of trouble

he will keep me safe in his dwelling.

PSALM 27:3-5 NIV

The humble will see their God at work and be glad.
Let all who seek God's help be encouraged.

PSALM 69:32 NLT

May the God who gives endurance and
encouragement give you the same attitude of mind
toward each other that Christ Jesus had.

ROMANS 15:5 NIV

We do not lose heart, but though our outer man is
decaying, yet our inner man is being renewed day by day.
For momentary, light affliction is producing for us an
eternal weight of glory far beyond all comparison.

2 CORINTHIANS 4:16–17 NASB

Let us consider how to stir up one another to love and
good works, not neglecting to meet together, as is the
habit of some, but encouraging one another.

HEBREWS 10:24–25 ESV

I am Enriched

GOD's blessing makes life rich;

nothing we do can improve on God.

PROVERBS 10:22 MSG

Oh, the depth of the riches both of the wisdom

and knowledge of God! How unsearchable are

His judgments and unfathomable His ways!

ROMANS 11:33 NASB

Every good gift and every perfect gift is from above,

coming down from the Father of lights with whom

there is no variation or shadow due to change.

JAMES 1:17 ESV

Everything God created is good, and nothing is to be

rejected if it is received with thanksgiving.

1 TIMOTHY 4:4 NIV

I will tell of the kindnesses of the LORD,

the deeds for which he is to be praised,

according to all the LORD has done for us...

according to his compassion and many kindnesses.

ISAIAH 63:7 NIV

A good man's speech reveals the rich treasures within him.

MATTHEW 12:35 TLB

Blessed are those who find wisdom,

those who gain understanding,

for she is more profitable than silver

and yields better returns than gold.

She is more precious than rubies;

nothing you desire can compare with her.

Long life is in her right hand;

in her left hand are riches and honor.

Her ways are pleasant ways,

and all her paths are peace.

PROVERBS 3:13–17 NIV

I am Enthusiastic

Work with enthusiasm, as though you were working
for the Lord rather than for people.

EPHESIANS 6:7 NLT

We should make the most of what God gives,
both the bounty and the capacity to enjoy it, accepting
what's given and delighting in the work. It's God's gift!

ECCLESIASTES 5:19 MSG

By You I can run against a troop,
By my God I can leap over a wall.

PSALM 18:29 NKJV

Whatever your hand finds to do, do it with all your might.

ECCLESIASTES 9:10 NIV

Everything else is worthless when compared with the
priceless gain of knowing Christ Jesus my Lord.
I have put aside all else, counting it worth less than
nothing, in order that I can have Christ…. Now I have
given up everything else—I have found it to be the only
way to really know Christ and to experience the mighty
power that brought him back to life again, and to find out
what it means to suffer and to die with him. So whatever
it takes, I will be one who lives in the fresh newness of life
of those who are alive from the dead.

PHILIPPIANS 3:8,10-11 TLB

I am Equipped

All scripture is inspired by God and is useful for
teaching, for reproof, for correction, and for training in
righteousness, so that everyone who belongs to God may
be proficient, equipped for every good work.

2 TIMOTHY 3:16–17 NRSV

May He give you the power to accomplish all
the good things your faith prompts you to do.

2 THESSALONIANS 1:11 NLT

Then the LORD reached out his hand and touched
my mouth and said to me, "I have put my words
in your mouth."

JEREMIAH 1:9 NIV

We are God's handiwork, created in Christ Jesus to do
good works, which God prepared in advance for us to do.

EPHESIANS 2:10 NIV

So then, my beloved, just as you have always obeyed,
not as in my presence only, but now much more in my
absence, work out your salvation with fear and trembling;
for it is God who is at work in you, both to will and to
work for His good pleasure.

PHILIPPIANS 2:12-13 NASB

If any of you lacks wisdom, you should ask God,
who gives generously to all without finding fault,
and it will be given to you.

JAMES 1:5 NIV

I am Forgiven

For You, Lord, are good, and ready to forgive,
And abundant in mercy to all those who call upon You.

PSALM 86:5 NKJV

Whenever you stand praying, forgive, if you have anything
against anyone, so that your Father also who is in heaven
may forgive you.

MARK 11:25 ESV

As far as the east is from the west,
So far has He removed our transgressions from us.

PSALM 103:12 NASB

If we confess our sins, He is faithful and just to forgive us
our sins and to cleanse us from all unrighteousness.

1 John 1:9 nkjv

He is so rich in kindness and grace that he purchased our
freedom with the blood of his Son and forgave our sins.

Ephesians 1:7 nlt

My sacrifice, O God, is a broken spirit;
a broken and contrite heart
you, God, will not despise.

Psalm 51:17 niv

Her sins—and they are many—have been forgiven,
so she has shown me much love. But a person who
is forgiven little shows only little love.

Luke 7:47 nlt

If you forgive other people when they sin against you,
your heavenly Father will also forgive you.

Matthew 6:14 niv

I am Free

Now that you have been set free from sin and have
become slaves of God, the benefit you reap leads to
holiness, and the result is eternal life.

ROMANS 6:22 NIV

Jesus said, "If you hold to my teaching,
you are really my disciples. Then you will know the truth,
and the truth will set you free."

JOHN 8:31–32 NIV

So Christ has truly set us free. Now make sure that you
stay free, and don't get tied up again in slavery to the law.

GALATIANS 5:1 NLT

He has delivered us from the power of darkness and
conveyed us into the kingdom of the Son of His love.

COLOSSIANS 1:13 NKJV

There is now no condemnation for those who are in
Christ Jesus, because through Christ Jesus
the law of the Spirit who gives life has
set you free from the law of sin and death.

ROMANS 8:1–2 NIV

Understand what we are telling you: You can have
forgiveness of your sins through Jesus. The law of Moses
could not free you from your sins. But through Jesus
everyone who believes is free from all sins.

ACTS 13:38-39 NCV

Now the Lord is the Spirit, and where
the Spirit of the Lord is, there is freedom.

2 CORINTHIANS 3:17 NRSV

I am Generous

Let each one give as he purposes in his heart, not
grudgingly or of necessity; for God loves a cheerful giver.

2 CORINTHIANS 9:7 NKJV

It is more blessed to give than to receive.

ACTS 20:35 NIV

One man gives freely, yet gains even more;
another withholds unduly, but comes to poverty.
A generous man will prosper;
whoever refreshes others will be refreshed.

PROVERBS 11:24–25 NIV

Whoever is generous to the poor lends to the Lord,
and he will repay him for his deed.

PROVERBS 19:17 ESV

When you give to the needy, do not let your left hand
know what your right hand is doing, so that
your giving may be in secret. Then your Father,
who sees what is done in secret, will reward you.

MATTHEW 6:3–4 NIV

You shall generously give to him, and your heart
shall not be grieved when you give to him,
because for this thing the Lord your God will bless you
in all your work and in all your undertakings.

DEUTERONOMY 15:10 NASB

The generous will themselves be blessed,
for they share their food with the poor.

PROVERBS 22:9 NIV

I am Gentle

A gentle answer deflects anger,
but harsh words make tempers flare.

PROVERBS 15:1 NLT

In your hearts revere Christ as Lord.
Always be prepared to give an answer to everyone who
asks you to give the reason for the hope that you have.
But do this with gentleness and respect.

1 PETER 3:15 NIV

Remind the believers to yield to the authority of rulers
and government leaders, to obey them, to be ready to
do good, to speak no evil about anyone, to live in peace,
and to be gentle and polite to all people.

TITUS 3:1-2 NCV

The wisdom that comes from heaven is first of all pure
and full of quiet gentleness. Then it is peace-loving
and courteous. It allows discussion and is willing
to yield to others; it is full of mercy and good deeds.
It is wholehearted and straightforward and sincere.

JAMES 3:17 TLB

Blessed are the gentle, for they shall inherit the earth.

MATTHEW 5:5 NASB

Let your gentleness be evident to all. The Lord is near.

PHILIPPIANS 4:5 NIV

You have given me the shield of your salvation,
and your right hand supported me,
and your gentleness made me great.

PSALM 18:35 ESV

I am Guided

Whether you turn to the right or to the left,
your ears will hear a voice behind you, saying,
"This is the way; walk in it."

We can make our plans,
but the Lord determines our steps.

PROVERBS 16:9 NLT

Guide me in your truth and teach me,
for you are God my Savior,
and my hope is in you all day long.

PSALM 25:5 NIV

The true children of God are those who let
God's Spirit lead them.

ROMANS 8:14 NCV

Trust in the LORD with all your heart,
And lean not on your own understanding;
In all your ways acknowledge Him,
And He shall direct your paths.

PROVERBS 3:5–6 NKJV

We ask God to give you complete knowledge of his will
and to give you spiritual wisdom and understanding.
Then the way you live will always honor and please the
Lord, and your lives will produce every kind of good fruit.
All the while, you will grow as you learn to know
God better and better.

COLOSSIANS 1:9–10 NLT

Listen to advice and accept discipline,
and at the end you will be counted among the wise.

PROVERBS 19:20 NIV

I am Happy

Happy are those who hear the joyful call to worship,
for they will walk in the light of your presence, Lord.

Psalm 89:15 nlt

May you be filled with joy, always thanking the Father. He
has enabled you to share in the inheritance that belongs to
his people, who live in the light.

Colossians 1:11–12 nlt

Enter his gates with thanksgiving,
and his courts with praise.
Give thanks to him, bless his name.
For the Lord is good;
his steadfast love endures forever,
and his faithfulness to all generations.

Psalm 100:4–5 nrsv

He will yet fill your mouth with laughter
and your lips with shouts of joy.

The Lord has done great things for us,
and we are filled with joy.

PSALM 126:3 NIV

I know that there is nothing better for people than to be
happy and to do good while they live.

ECCLESIASTES 3:12 NIV

I will give thanks to the LORD with my whole heart;
I will recount all of your wonderful deeds.
I will be glad and exult in you;
I will sing praise to your name, O Most High.

PSALM 9:1-2 ESV

Rejoice in the Lord always. Again I will say, rejoice!

PHILIPPIANS 4:4 NKJV

I am Healed

Trust God from the bottom of your heart;

don't try to figure out everything on your own.

Listen for God's voice in everything you do,

everywhere you go;

he's the one who will keep you on track.

Don't assume that you know it all.

Run to God! Run from evil!

Your body will glow with health,

your very bones will vibrate with life!

PROVERBS 3:5–8 MSG

He was pierced for our transgressions,

he was crushed for our iniquities;

the punishment that brought us peace was on him,

and by his wounds we are healed.

ISAIAH 53:5 NIV

A cheerful heart does good like medicine.

PROVERBS 17:22 TLB

Daughter, your faith has made you well;
go in peace and be healed of your affliction.

MARK 5:34 NASB

My child, pay attention to what I say.
Listen carefully to my words.
Don't lose sight of them.
Let them penetrate deep into your heart,
for they bring life to those who find them,
and healing to their whole body.

PROVERBS 4:20–22 NLT

The world and its desires pass away,
but whoever does the will of God lives forever.

1 JOHN 2:17 NIV

I am Heaven-bound

We fix our eyes not on what is seen,

but on what is unseen, since what is seen is temporary,

but what is unseen is eternal.

2 Corinthians 4:18 niv

Before the mountains were brought forth,

or ever you had formed the earth and the world,

from everlasting to everlasting you are God.

Psalm 90:2 esv

Surely goodness and mercy shall follow me

All the days of my life;

And I will dwell in the house of the Lord

Forever.

Psalm 23:6 nkjv

We are citizens of heaven, where the Lord Jesus Christ lives.
And we are eagerly waiting for him to return as our Savior.
He will take our weak mortal bodies and change them into
glorious bodies like his own, using the same power with
which he will bring everything under his control.

PHILIPPIANS 3:20–21 NLT

I'm asking GOD for one thing,
only one thing:
To live with him in his house
my whole life long.
I'll contemplate his beauty;
I'll study at his feet.

PSALM 27:4 MSG

I will come back and take you to be with me that you also
may be where I am.

JOHN 14:3 NIV

I am Hopeful

God...rekindles burned-out lives with fresh hope,

Restoring dignity and respect to their lives—

a place in the sun!

1 Samuel 2:7–8 msg

Blessed be the God and Father of our Lord Jesus Christ!

According to his great mercy, he has caused us to be born

again to a living hope through the resurrection of Jesus Christ.

1 Peter 1:3 esv

The Lord is good to those whose hope is in him,

to the one who seeks him.

Lamentations 3:25 niv

There is surely a future hope for you,
and your hope will not be cut off.

PROVERBS 23:18 NIV

We can rejoice, too, when we run into problems and trials,
for we know that they help us develop endurance. And
endurance develops strength of character, and character
strengthens our confident hope of salvation. And this
hope will not lead to disappointment. For we know how
dearly God loves us, because he has given us the Holy
Spirit to fill our hearts with his love.

ROMANS 5:3–5 NLT

May the God of hope fill you with all joy and
peace as you trust in him, so that you may overflow
with hope by the power of the Holy Spirit.

ROMANS 15:13 NIV

I am Humble

Humility is the fear of the LORD;
its wages are riches and honor and life.

PROVERBS 22:4 NIV

Where you have envy and selfish ambition, there you
find disorder and every evil practice. But the wisdom that
comes from heaven is first of all pure; then peace-loving,
considerate, submissive, full of mercy and good fruit,
impartial and sincere. Peacemakers who sow in peace reap
a harvest of righteousness.

JAMES 3:16–18 NIV

Those who accept correction gain understanding.
Respect for the LORD will teach you wisdom.
If you want to be honored, you must be humble.

PROVERBS 15:32–33 NCV

In your relationships with one another, have the same
mindset as Christ Jesus:
Who, being in very nature God,
did not consider equality with God something
to be used to his own advantage;
rather, he made himself nothing
by taking the very nature of a servant,
being made in human likeness.
And being found in appearance as a man,
he humbled himself
by becoming obedient to death—
even death on a cross!
Therefore God exalted him to the highest place
and gave him the name that is above every name.

PHILIPPIANS 2:5–9 NIV

I am Inspired

The precepts of the LORD are right,

giving joy to the heart.

The commands of the LORD are radiant,

giving light to the eyes.

PSALM 19:8 NIV

I am the Light of the world; he who follows Me will not

walk in the darkness, but will have the Light of life.

JOHN 8:12 NASB

Your laws are my treasure; they are my heart's delight.

PSALM 119:111 NLT

Pursue a righteous life—a life of wonder, faith, love, steadiness, courtesy. Run hard and fast in the faith. Seize the eternal life, the life you were called to, the life you so fervently embraced in the presence of so many witnesses.

1 Timothy 6:11–12 MSG

I have been crucified with Christ;
and it is no longer I who live,
but Christ lives in me.

Galatians 2:20 NASB

You are the light of the world. A city set on a hill
cannot be hidden. Nor do people light a lamp
and put it under a basket, but on a stand,
and it gives light to all in the house. In the same way,
let your light shine before others, so that they may
see your good works and give glory to your
Father who is in heaven.

Matthew 5:14–16 ESV

I am Joyful

Satisfy us in the morning with your unfailing love,
that we may sing for joy and be glad all our days.

PSALM 90:14 NIV

Be truly glad. There is wonderful joy ahead....
You love him even though you have never seen him.
Though you do not see him now, you trust him;
and you rejoice with a glorious, inexpressible joy.

1 PETER 1:6, 8 NLT

Until now you have not asked for anything in my name.
Ask and you will receive, and your joy will be complete.

JOHN 16:24 NIV

Let all those rejoice who put their trust in You;

Let them ever shout for joy, because You defend them;

Let those also who love Your name

Be joyful in You.

PSALM 5:11 NKJV

Our mouth was filled with laughter,

and our tongue with shouts of joy.

PSALM 126:2 ESV

I have told you this so that my joy may be in you

and that your joy may be complete.

JOHN 15:11 NIV

You will go out in joy

and be led forth in peace;

the mountains and hills

will burst into song before you,

and all the trees of the field

will clap their hands.

ISAIAH 55:12 NIV

I am Known

God's solid foundation stands firm, sealed with this
inscription: "The Lord knows those who are his."

2 TIMOTHY 2:19 NIV

When I was a child, I spoke and thought and reasoned as
a child. But when I grew up, I put away childish things.
Now we see things imperfectly, like puzzling reflections
in a mirror, but then we will see everything with perfect
clarity. All that I know now is partial and incomplete, but
then I will know everything completely, just as God now
knows me completely.

1 CORINTHIANS 13:11-12 NLT

"For I know the plans I have for you," declares the Lord,

"plans to prosper you and not to harm you,

plans to give you hope and a future."

Jeremiah 29:11 niv

I will instruct you and teach you in the way you should go;

I will counsel you with my loving eye on you.

Psalm 32:8 niv

O Lord, You have searched me and known me.

You know my sitting down and my rising up;

You understand my thought afar off.

You comprehend my path and my lying down,

And are acquainted with all my ways.

For there is not a word on my tongue,

But behold, Lord, You know it altogether.

Psalm 139:1–4 nkjv

I am Loved

The steadfast love of the LORD never ceases;

his mercies never come to an end;

they are new every morning;

great is your faithfulness.

LAMENTATIONS 3:22–23 ESV

Know therefore that the LORD your God is God;

he is the faithful God, keeping his covenant of love

to a thousand generations of those who love him

and keep his commandments.

DEUTERONOMY 7:9 NIV

Let love and faithfulness never leave you;

bind them around your neck,

write them on the tablet of your heart.

PROVERBS 3:3 NIV

We have come to know and have believed the love
which God has for us. God is love, and the one who
abides in love abides in God, and God abides in him.
We love, because He first loved us.

1 John 4:16, 19 NASB

You, O Lord, are good and forgiving,
abounding in steadfast love to all who call upon you.

Psalm 86:5 ESV

Three things will last forever—faith, hope, and love—
and the greatest of these is love.

1 Corinthians 13:13 NLT

I will sing of the Lord's great love forever;
with my mouth I will make your faithfulness known
through all generations.
I will declare that your love stands firm forever,
that you have established your faithfulness in heaven itself.

Psalm 89:1–2 NIV

I am Pardoned

Where is another God like you, who pardons the sins
of the survivors among his people? You cannot
stay angry with your people, for you love to be merciful.
Once again you will have compassion on us. You will tread
our sins beneath your feet; you will throw them into
the depths of the ocean! You will bless us as you
promised Jacob long ago. You will set your love upon us,
as you promised our father Abraham!

MICAH 7:18–20 TLB

Sin shall no longer be your master,
because you are not under the law, but under grace.

ROMANS 6:14 NIV

He gives more grace. Therefore He says:

"God resists the proud,

But gives grace to the humble."

JAMES 4:6 NKJV

God is so rich in mercy, and he loved us so much,

that even though we were dead because of our sins,

he gave us life when he raised Christ from the dead.

(It is only by God's grace that you have been saved!)…

God saved you by his grace when you believed.

And you can't take credit for this; it is a gift from God.

Salvation is not a reward for the good things we have

done, so none of us can boast about it.

EPHESIANS 2:4–5, 8–9 NLT

I am Patient

The LORD longs to be gracious to you;
therefore he will rise up to show you compassion.
For the LORD is a God of justice.
Blessed are all who wait for him!

ISAIAH 30:18 NIV

The Lord isn't really being slow about his promise,
as some people think. No, he is being patient
for your sake. He does not want anyone to be destroyed,
but wants everyone to repent.

2 PETER 3:9 NLT

As a prisoner for the Lord, then, I urge you to
live a life worthy of the calling you have received.
Be completely humble and gentle; be patient,
bearing with one another in love.

EPHESIANS 4:1-2 NIV

They are those who, hearing the word, hold it fast in an
honest and good heart, and bear fruit with patience.

LUKE 8:15 ESV

We are saved by trusting. And trusting means looking
forward to getting something we don't yet have—
for a man who already has something doesn't need
to hope and trust that he will get it. But if we must keep
trusting God for something that hasn't happened yet,
it teaches us to wait patiently and confidently.

ROMANS 8:24-25 TLB

Imitate those who through faith and patience
inherit what has been promised.

HEBREWS 6:12 NIV

I am Peaceful

These things I have spoken to you, so that in Me you
may have peace. In the world you have tribulation,
but take courage; I have overcome the world.

JOHN 16:33 NASB

The LORD will give strength to His people;
The LORD will bless His people with peace.

PSALM 29:11 NKJV

Peace I leave with you; my peace I give you.
I do not give to you as the world gives.
Do not let your hearts be troubled and do not be afraid.

JOHN 14:27 NIV

If people's thinking is controlled by the sinful self, there is death. But if their thinking is controlled by the Spirit, there is life and peace.

Romans 8:6 ncv

Those who love your instructions have great peace and do not stumble.

Psalm 119:165 nlt

God is not a God of confusion but of peace.

1 Corinthians 14:33 nasb

Let the peace of Christ rule in your hearts, since as members of one body you were called to peace.

Colossians 3:15 niv

May the Lord of peace himself give you peace at all times and in every way. The Lord be with all of you.

2 Thessalonians 3:16 niv

I am Perceptive

The unfolding of your words gives light;
it gives understanding to the simple.

PSALM 119:130 NIV

What we have received is not the spirit of the world,
but the Spirit who is from God, so that we may understand
what God has freely given us.

1 CORINTHIANS 2:12 NIV

Do not be unwise, but understand what
the will of the Lord is.

EPHESIANS 5:17 NKJV

Do not let wisdom and understanding out of your sight,
preserve sound judgment and discretion;
they will be life for you.

PROVERBS 3:21-22 NIV

Be filled with the knowledge of His will in all spiritual

wisdom and understanding, so that you will walk in

a manner worthy of the Lord… and increasing in the

knowledge of God.

COLOSSIANS 1:9-10 NASB

The wisdom from above is first of all pure.

It is also peace loving, gentle at all times, and willing

to yield to others. It is full of mercy and good deeds.

It shows no favoritism and is always sincere.

JAMES 3:17 NLT

Listen carefully to wisdom;

set your mind on understanding.

Cry out for wisdom,

and beg for understanding.

Search for it like silver,

and hunt for it like hidden treasure.

Then you will understand respect for the LORD,

and you will find that you know God.

PROVERBS 2:2-5 NCV

I am Persevering

God blesses those who patiently endure testing and
temptation. Afterward they will receive the crown of life
that God has promised to those who love him.

JAMES 1:12 NLT

Let us not grow weary of doing good, for in due season
we will reap, if we do not give up.

GALATIANS 6:9 ESV

Wait on the LORD;
Be of good courage,
And He shall strengthen your heart;
Wait, I say, on the LORD!

PSALM 27:14 NKJV

The one who endures to the end will be saved.

MATTHEW 24:13 ESV

Consider it pure joy...whenever you face trials
of many kinds, because you know that the testing
of your faith develops perseverance. Let perseverance
finish its work so that you may be mature
and complete, not lacking anything.

JAMES 1:2–4 NIV

Since we are surrounded by such a great cloud of
witnesses, let us throw off everything that hinders and
the sin that so easily entangles. And let us run with
perseverance the race marked out for us, fixing our eyes on
Jesus....so that you will not grow weary and lose heart.

HEBREWS 12:1–3 NIV

May the Lord direct your hearts into God's love
and Christ's perseverance.

2 THESSALONIANS 3:5 NIV

I am Prayerful

My voice You shall hear in the morning, O Lord;
In the morning I will direct it to You,
And I will look up.

PSALM 5:3 NKJV

Ask and it will be given to you; seek and you will find;
knock and the door will be opened to you. For everyone
who asks receives; he who seeks finds; and to him who
knocks, the door will be opened.

MATTHEW 7:7–8 NIV

I call on you, My God, for you will answer me;
turn your ear to me and hear my prayer.

PSALM 17:6 NIV

The prayer of a righteous person is powerful and effective.

JAMES 5:16 NIV

The Spirit also helps our weakness; for we do not
know how to pray as we should, but the Spirit Himself
intercedes for us with groanings too deep for words.

ROMANS 8:26 NASB

Pray without ceasing.

1 THESSALONIANS 5:17 NKJV

You, God, are my God,
earnestly I seek you;
I thirst for you,
my whole being longs for you,
in a dry and parched land
where there is no water.

PSALM 63:1 NIV

With all prayer and petition pray at all times in the Spirit,
and with this in view, be on the alert with
all perseverance and petition for all the saints.

EPHESIANS 6:18 NASB

I am Protected

The LORD himself goes before you and will be with you;

he will never leave you nor forsake you.

DEUTERONOMY 31:8 NIV

If you make the LORD your refuge,

if you make the Most High your shelter,

no evil will conquer you;

no plague will come near your home.

For he will order his angels

to protect you wherever you go.

PSALM 91:9–11 NLT

How great is the goodness

you have stored up for those who fear you.

You lavish it on those who come to you for protection,

blessing them before the watching world.

PSALM 31:19 NLT

The Lord is faithful, and he will
strengthen you and protect you.

2 Thessalonians 3:3 niv

The Lord will keep you from all harm—
he will watch over your life;
the Lord will watch over your coming and going
both now and forevermore.

Psalm 121:7–8 niv

But let all who take refuge in you be glad;
let them ever sing for joy.
Spread your protection over them,
that those who love your name may rejoice in you.

Psalm 5:11 niv

But you, Lord, do not be far from me.
You are my strength; come quickly to help me.

Psalm 22:19 niv

I am Pure

Our faces, then, are not covered. We all show the Lord's
glory, and we are being changed to be like him.
This change in us brings ever greater glory,
which comes from the Lord, who is the Spirit.

2 CORINTHIANS 3:18 NCV

Teach me your ways, O LORD,
that I may live according to your truth!
Grant me purity of heart,
so that I may honor you.

PSALM 86:11 NLT

Now that you have purified yourselves by obeying
the truth so that you have sincere love for each other,
love one another deeply, from the heart.

1 PETER 1:22 NIV

Examine everything carefully; hold fast to that which is good; abstain from every form of evil.

Whatever is true, whatever is honorable, whatever is just, whatever is pure, whatever is lovely, whatever is commendable, if there is any excellence, if there is anything worthy of praise, think about these things.

Do everything without grumbling or arguing, so that you may become blameless and pure, "children of God without fault in a warped and crooked generation." Then you will shine among them like stars in the sky as you hold firmly to the word of life.

To do what is right and just is more acceptable to the Lord than sacrifice.

I am Reconciled

You were separate from Christ...foreigners to the
covenants of the promise, without hope and without God
in the world. But now in Christ Jesus you who once were
far away have been brought near by the blood of Christ.

EPHESIANS 2:12–13 NIV

We are made right with God by placing our faith in
Jesus Christ. And this is true for everyone who believes,
no matter who we are. For everyone has sinned;
we all fall short of God's glorious standard.
Yet God, with undeserved kindness, declares that
we are righteous. He did this through Christ Jesus
when he freed us from the penalty for our sins.

ROMANS 3:22–24 NLT

We have stopped evaluating others from a human point of view. At one time we thought of Christ merely from a human point of view. How differently we know him now! This means that anyone who belongs to Christ has become a new person. The old life is gone; a new life has begun! And all of this is a gift from God, who brought us back to himself through Christ. And God has given us this task of reconciling people to him.

2 CORINTHIANS 5:16–18 NLT

I am Redeemed

By entering through faith into what God has always
wanted to do for us—set us right with him, make us fit
for him—we have it all together with God because of
our Master Jesus. And that's not all: We throw open our
doors to God and discover at the same moment that he
has already thrown open his door to us. We find ourselves
standing where we always hoped we might stand—out in
the wide open spaces of God's grace and glory, standing
tall and shouting our praise.

ROMANS 5:1–2 MSG

Be gracious to me, O God,

according to Your lovingkindness;

According to the greatness of Your compassion

blot out my transgressions.

PSALM 51:1 NASB

Once you were dead because of your disobedience and

your many sins.... All of us used to live that way, following

the passionate desires and inclinations of our sinful

nature. By our very nature we were subject to God's anger,

just like everyone else. But God is so rich in mercy,

and he loved us so much, that even though we

were dead because of our sins, he gave us life

when he raised Christ from the dead.

EPHESIANS 2:1, 3–5 NLT

I am Refreshed

The law of the LORD is perfect,

refreshing the soul.

The statutes of the LORD are trustworthy,

making wise the simple.

PSALM 19:7 NIV

Jesus replied that people soon became thirsty again after

drinking this water. "But the water I give them," he said,

"becomes a perpetual spring within them, watering them

forever with eternal life."

JOHN 4:13-14 TLB

A generous person will prosper;

whoever refreshes others will be refreshed.

PROVERBS 11: 25 NIV

Jesus stood and said…"Let anyone who is thirsty come to

me and drink. Whoever believes in me, as Scripture has

said, rivers of living water will flow from within them."

JOHN 7:37–38 NIV

Your love, LORD, reaches to the heavens,

your faithfulness to the skies.

Your righteousness is like the highest mountains,

your justice like the great deep.

You, LORD, preserve both people and animals.

How priceless is your unfailing love, O God!

People take refuge in the shadow of your wings.

They feast on the abundance of your house;

you give them drink from your river of delights.

For with you is the fountain of life;

in your light we see light.

PSALM 36:5–9 NIV

I am Renewed

We shall not all sleep, but we shall all be changed.

1 CORINTHIANS 15:51 NKJV

The LORD is good to all,
and his mercy is over all that he has made.

PSALM 145:9 ESV

When you were stuck in your old sin-dead life, you were
incapable of responding to God. God brought you alive—
right along with Christ! Think of it! All sins forgiven, the
slate wiped clean, that old arrest warrant canceled and
nailed to Christ's cross.

COLOSSIANS 2:13 MSG

If anyone is in Christ, he is a new creation; old things have
passed away; behold, all things have become new.

2 CORINTHIANS 5:17 NKJV

Praise the LORD!
Oh, give thanks to the LORD, for He is good!
For His mercy endures forever.

PSALM 106:1 NKJV

God put the world square with himself through the
Messiah, giving the world a fresh start by offering
forgiveness of sins. God has given us the task of telling
everyone what he is doing. We're Christ's representatives.
God uses us to persuade men and women to drop their
differences and enter into God's work of making things
right between them. We're speaking for Christ himself now:
Become friends with God; he's already a friend with you.

2 CORINTHIANS 5:19–20 MSG

I am Restored

Since we have been made right in God's sight by faith,
we have peace with God because of what Jesus Christ
our Lord has done for us. Because of our faith,
Christ has brought us into this place of undeserved
privilege where we now stand, and we confidently and
joyfully look forward to sharing God's glory.

ROMANS 5:1–2 NLT

He has saved us and called us to a holy life—
not because of anything we have done
but because of his own purpose and grace.

2 TIMOTHY 1:9 NIV

Dear brothers and sisters, we can boldly enter heaven's
Most Holy Place because of the blood of Jesus. By his
death, Jesus opened a new and life-giving way through the
curtain into the Most Holy Place. And since we
have a great High Priest who rules over God's house,
let us go right into the presence of God with
sincere hearts fully trusting him.

Hebrews 10:19–22 nlt

Let us praise the Lord, the God of Israel,
because he has come to help his people and has given
them freedom.
He has given us a powerful Savior.

Luke 1:68-69 ncv

I am Rewarded

Without faith it is impossible to please God, because
anyone who comes to him must believe that he exists and
that he rewards those who earnestly seek him.

HEBREWS 11:6 NIV

Do not lose the courage you had in the past,
which has a great reward. You must hold on, so you can
do what God wants and receive what he has promised.

HEBREWS 10:35–36 NCV

Watch yourselves, so that you may not lose what
we have worked for, but may win a full reward.

2 JOHN 1:8 ESV

Look, I am coming soon! My reward is with me, and I will
give to each person according to what they have done.

Revelation 22:12 niv

Remember that the Lord will reward
each one of us for the good we do.

Ephesians 6:8 nlt

I have fought the good fight, I have finished the course,
I have kept the faith; in the future there is laid up for me
the crown of righteousness, which the Lord, the righteous
Judge, will award to me on that day; and not only to me,
but also to all who have loved His appearing.

2 Timothy 4:7-8 nasb

I am Royalty

Because we are his children, God has sent the
Spirit of his Son into our hearts, prompting us
to call out, "Abba, Father." Now you are no longer
a slave but God's own child. And since you are his child,
God has made you his heir.

GALATIANS 4:6-7 NLT

As many as received Him, to them He gave
the right to become children of God,
even to those who believe in His name.

JOHN 1:12 NASB

See what great love the Father has lavished on us,
that we should be called children of God!
And that is what we are! The reason the world does not
know us is that it did not know him. Dear friends, now we
are children of God, and what we will be has not yet been
made known. But we know that when Christ appears, we
shall be like him, for we shall see him as he is.

1 John 3:1-2 NIV

Love your enemies, do good to them, and lend to them
without expecting to get anything back. Then your reward
will be great, and you will be children of the Most High.

Luke 6:35 NIV

I am Satisfied

Because your love is better than life,

my lips will glorify you.

I will praise you as long as I live,

and in your name I will lift up my hands.

I will be fully satisfied as with the richest of foods;

with singing lips my mouth will praise you.

PSALM 63:3–5 NIV

God is able to provide you with every blessing in

abundance, so that by always having enough of everything,

you may share abundantly in every good work.

2 CORINTHIANS 9:8 NRSV

The LORD is all I need.

He takes care of me.

My share in life has been pleasant;

my part has been beautiful.

PSALM 16:5–6 NCV

The poor shall eat and be satisfied; all who see

the Lord shall find him and shall praise his name.

Their hearts shall rejoice with everlasting joy.

PSALM 22:26 TLB

Give, and it will be given to you.

A good measure, pressed down, shaken together

and running over, will be poured into your lap.

For with the measure you use,

it will be measured to you.

LUKE 6:38 NIV

Whoever pursues righteousness and love

finds life, prosperity and honor.

PROVERBS 21:21 NIV

I am Secure

The everlasting God is your place of safety,
and his arms will hold you up forever.

DEUTERONOMY 33:27 NCV

Every good and perfect gift is from above,
coming down from the Father of the heavenly lights,
who does not change like shifting shadows.

JAMES 1:17 NIV

You are near, LORD,
and all your commands are true.
Long ago I learned from your statutes
that you established them to last forever.

PSALM 119:151–152 NIV

The grass withers,

And its flower falls away,

But the word of the LORD endures forever.

1 PETER 1:24–25 NKJV

In peace I will lie down and sleep,

for you alone, LORD,

make me dwell in safety.

PSALM 4:8 NIV

When you go through deep waters and great trouble,

I will be with you. When you go through rivers

of difficulty, you will not drown! When you walk through

the fire of oppression, you will not be burned up—

the flames will not consume you.

ISAIAH 43:2 TLB

Our steps are made firm by the LORD,

when he delights in our way;

though we stumble, we shall not fall headlong,

for the LORD holds us by the hand.

PSALM 37:23–24 NRSV

I am Strong

Have you never heard?

Have you never understood?

The LORD is the everlasting God,

the Creator of all the earth.

He never grows weak or weary.

No one can measure the depths of his understanding.

He gives power to the weak

and strength to the powerless.

Even youths will become weak and tired,

and young men will fall in exhaustion.

But those who trust in the LORD will find new strength.

They will soar high on wings like eagles.

They will run and not grow weary.

They will walk and not faint.

ISAIAH 40:28-31 NLT

"My grace is sufficient for you, for My strength is made perfect in weakness." Therefore most gladly I will rather boast in my infirmities, that the power of Christ may rest upon me…. For when I am weak, then I am strong.

2 Corinthians 12:9 NKJV

In Your hand is power and might;
In Your hand it is to make great
And to give strength to all.

1 Chronicles 29:12 NKJV

Be strong in the Lord and in his mighty power.
Put on the full armor of God, so that you can
take your stand against the devil's schemes.

Ephesians 6:10–11 NIV

I am Supported

The Lord stood by me and gave me strength....
The Lord will rescue me from every evil attack
and save me for his heavenly kingdom.

2 TIMOTHY 4:17-18 NRSV

Whom have I in heaven but you?
And earth has nothing I desire besides you.
My flesh and my heart may fail,
but God is the strength of my heart
and my portion forever.

PSALM 73:25–26 NIV

The LORD is near to the brokenhearted
and saves the crushed in spirit.

PSALM 34:18 ESV

You, God, see the trouble of the afflicted;

you consider their grief and take it in hand.

The victims commit themselves to you;

you are the helper of the fatherless.

PSALM 10:14 NIV

Live as citizens of heaven, conducting yourselves in

a manner worthy of the Good News about Christ…

standing together with one spirit and one purpose,

fighting together for the faith. Don't be intimidated in any

way by your enemies. This will be a sign to them that you

are going to be saved, even by God himself.

PHILIPPIANS 1:27–28 NLT

God will never forget the needy;

the hope of the afflicted will never perish.

PSALM 9:18 NIV

You are my hiding place;

You shall preserve me from trouble;

You shall surround me with songs of deliverance.

PSALM 32:7 NKJV

I am Sure

Faith is confidence in what we hope for
and assurance about what we do not see.

HEBREWS 11:1 NIV

Not one word of all the good words which the LORD
your God spoke concerning you has failed; all have been
fulfilled for you, not one of them has failed.

JOSHUA 23:14 NASB

As we pray to our God and Father about you, we think of
your faithful work, your loving deeds, and the enduring
hope you have because of our Lord Jesus Christ.

1 THESSALONIANS 1:3 NLT

Faith comes by hearing, and hearing by the word of God.

ROMANS 10:17 NKJV

If you have faith like a grain of mustard seed, you will say
to this mountain, "Move from here to there," and it will
move, and nothing will be impossible for you.

MATTHEW 17:20 ESV

Through Christ you have come to trust in God. And you
have placed your faith and hope in God because he raised
Christ from the dead and gave him great glory.

1 PETER 1:21 NLT

Until heaven and earth disappear, not the smallest letter,
not the least stroke of a pen, will by any means disappear
from the Law until everything is accomplished.

MATTHEW 5:18 NIV

I am Sustained

God is able to bless you abundantly, so that
in all things at all times, having all that you need,
you will abound in every good work.

2 CORINTHIANS 9:8 NIV

The LORD is my shepherd, I shall not want.
He makes me lie down in green pastures;
he leads me beside still waters;
he restores my soul.

PSALM 23:1–3 NRSV

You're blessed when you're at the end of your rope.

With less of you there is more of God and his rule.

MATTHEW 5:3 MSG

I fall to my knees and pray to the Father, the Creator of
everything in heaven and on earth.
I pray that from his glorious, unlimited resources he will
empower you with inner strength through his Spirit. Then
Christ will make his home in your hearts as you trust in
him. Your roots will grow down into God's love and keep
you strong. And may you have the power to understand,
as all God's people should, how wide, how long, how high,
and how deep his love is. May you experience the love of
Christ, though it is too great to understand fully. Then
you will be made complete with all the fullness of life and
power that comes from God.

EPHESIANS 3:14–19 NLT

I am Thankful

That my soul may sing praise to You and not be silent.
O LORD my God, I will give thanks to You forever.

PSALM 30:12 NASB

Thanks be to God for his indescribable gift!

2 CORINTHIANS 9:15 NIV

Be filled with the Holy Spirit, singing psalms and hymns
and spiritual songs among yourselves, and making music
to the Lord in your hearts. And give thanks for everything
to God the Father in the name of our Lord Jesus Christ.

EPHESIANS 5:18–20 NLT

Give thanks to the LORD, for he is good.

His love endures forever.

PSALM 136:1 NIV

Always be thankful. Let the message about Christ, in all

its richness, fill your lives. Teach and counsel each other

with all the wisdom he gives. Sing psalms and hymns and

spiritual songs to God with thankful hearts. And whatever

you do or say, do it as a representative of the Lord Jesus,

giving thanks through him to God the Father.

COLOSSIANS 3:15-17 NLT

In everything give thanks; for this is God's will

for you in Christ Jesus.

1 THESSALONIANS 5:18 NASB

Now therefore, our God,

We thank You

And praise Your glorious name.

1 CHRONICLES 29:13 NKJV

I am Trustworthy

Listen, for I will speak of excellent things,

And from the opening of my lips will come right things;

For my mouth will speak truth.

PROVERBS 8:6–7 NKJV

One who is faithful in a very little is also faithful in much.

LUKE 16:10 ESV

You must remain faithful to the things you have been taught.

You know they are true, for you know you can trust those

who taught you. You have been taught the holy Scriptures

from childhood, and they have given you the wisdom to

receive the salvation that comes by trusting in Christ Jesus.

2 TIMOTHY 3:14–15 NLT

The LORD detests lying lips,
but he delights in people who are trustworthy.

PROVERBS 12:22 NIV

A gossip goes around telling secrets,
but those who are trustworthy can keep a confidence.

PROVERBS 11:13 NLT

Show yourself in all respects to be a model of good works,
and in your teaching show integrity, dignity, and sound
speech that cannot be condemned, so that an opponent
may be put to shame, having nothing evil to say about us.

TITUS 2:7-8 ESV

Love and truth form a good leader;
sound leadership is founded on loving integrity.

PROVERBS 20:28 MSG

I am Truthful

Truthful words stand the test of time,

but lies are soon exposed.

PROVERBS 12:19 NLT

When he, the Spirit of truth, comes,

he will guide you into all the truth.

JOHN 16:13 NIV

You desire truth in the innermost being,

And in the hidden part You will make me know wisdom.

PSALM 51:6 NASB

Let us not love with words or speech

but with actions and in truth.

1 JOHN 3:18 NIV

The very essence of your words is truth;

all your just regulations will stand forever.

Psalm 119:160 nlt

Everyone who does evil hates the light, and will not come

into the light for fear that their deeds will be exposed.

But whoever lives by the truth comes into the light,

so that it may be seen plainly that what they have

done has been done in the sight of God.

John 3:20–21 niv

His merciful kindness is great toward us,

And the truth of the Lord endures forever.

Praise the Lord!

Psalm 117:2 nkjv

Send out your light and your truth;

let them lead me;

let them bring me to your holy hill

and to your dwelling.

Psalm 43:3 nrsv

I am Unafraid

There is no room in love for fear. Well-formed love banishes
fear. Since fear is crippling, a fearful life—fear of death, fear
of judgment—is one not yet fully formed in love.

1 JOHN 4:18 MSG

Don't be afraid, for I am with you.
Don't be discouraged, for I am your God.
I will strengthen you and help you.
I will hold you up with my victorious right hand.

ISAIAH 41:10 NLT

God has not given us a spirit of fear,
but of power and of love and of a sound mind.

2 TIMOTHY 1:7 NKJV

The LORD is my light and my salvation;
whom shall I fear?
The LORD is the stronghold of my life;
of whom shall I be afraid?

PSALM 27:1 ESV

Say to those with fearful hearts,
"Be strong, and do not fear,
for your God...is coming to save you."

ISAIAH 35:4 NLT

When you lie down, you will not be afraid;
when you lie down, your sleep will be sweet.
Have no fear of sudden disaster
or of the ruin that overtakes the wicked,
for the LORD will be at your side
and will keep your foot from being snared.

PROVERBS 3:24–26 NIV

I am Understood

You know what I long for, Lord;

you hear my every sigh.

PSALM 38:9 NLT

My sheep hear my voice, and I know them, and they
follow me. I give them eternal life, and they will never
perish, and no one will snatch them out of my hand.

JOHN 10:27-28 ESV

God is not unjust; he will not overlook your work and the
love that you showed for his sake in
serving the saints, as you still do.

HEBREWS 6:10 NRSV

Your Father knows what you need before you ask Him.

MATTHEW 6:8 NASB

Great is our Lord and mighty in power;
his understanding has no limit.

PSALM 147:5 NIV

For we do not have a high priest who is unable to empathize
with our weaknesses, but we have one who has been
tempted in every way, just as we are—yet he did not sin.

HEBREWS 4:15 NIV

As the heavens are higher than the earth,
So are My ways higher than your ways
And My thoughts higher than your thoughts.

ISAIAH 55:9 NASB

Blessed is the one who finds wisdom,
and the one who gets understanding.

PROVERBS 3:13 ESV

Our purpose is to please God, not people. He alone
examines the motives of our hearts.

1 THESSALONIANS 2:4 NLT

I am Untroubled

Blessed is the one who trusts in the Lord,

whose confidence is in him.

They will be like a tree planted by the water

that sends out its roots by the stream.

It does not fear when heat comes;

its leaves are always green.

It has no worries in a year of drought

and never fails to bear fruit.

JEREMIAH 17:7–8 NIV

Let not your heart be troubled; you believe in God, believe also in Me. In My Father's house are many mansions.... I go to prepare a place for you. And if I go and prepare a place for you, I will come again and receive you to Myself; that where I am, there you may be also.

JOHN 14:1-3 NKJV

Give your entire attention to what God is doing right now, and don't get worked up about what may or may not happen tomorrow. God will help you deal with whatever hard things come up when the time comes.

MATTHEW 6:34 MSG

Those who love me, I will deliver;
I will protect those who know my name.
When they call to me, I will answer them;
I will be with them in trouble,
I will rescue them and honor them.

PSALM 91:14-15 NRSV

I am Unwavering

Be attentive to my words;

incline your ear to my sayings.

Let them not escape from your sight;

keep them within your heart.

Let your eyes look directly forward,

and your gaze be straight before you.

PROVERBS 4:20–21, 25 ESV

Let us draw near to God with a sincere heart and with the

full assurance that faith brings....Let us hold unswervingly

to the hope we profess, for he who promised is faithful.

HEBREWS 10:22-23 NIV

Your lovingkindness, O LORD, extends to the heavens,

Your faithfulness reaches to the skies.

PSALM 36:5 NASB

God is faithful. He will not allow the temptation to be
more than you can stand. When you are tempted,
he will show you a way out so that you can endure.

1 Corinthians 10:13 nlt

I keep my eyes always on the Lord.
With him at my right hand, I will not be shaken.

Psalm 16:8 niv

Lord, you are my God;
I will exalt you and praise your name,
for in perfect faithfulness
you have done wonderful things,
things planned long ago.

Isaiah 25:1 niv

The word of the Lord is upright,
and all his work is done in faithfulness.

Psalm 33:4 esv

I am Unworried

Which of you by worrying can add
a single hour to his life's span?

LUKE 12:25 NASB

Don't worry about anything; instead, pray about
everything. Tell God what you need, and thank him for all
he has done. Then you will experience God's peace, which
exceeds anything we can understand. His peace will guard
your hearts and minds as you live in Christ Jesus.

PHILIPPIANS 4:6–7 NLT

Worry weighs a person down;
an encouraging word cheers a person up.

PROVERBS 12:25 NLT

Give your burdens to the LORD,

and he will take care of you.

PSALM 55:22 NLT

Do not worry about your life, what you will eat or drink;

or about your body, what you will wear. Is not life more

than food, and the body more than clothes? Look at the

birds of the air; they do not sow or reap or store away in

barns, and yet your heavenly Father feeds them. Are you

not much more valuable than they?

MATTHEW 6:25–26 NIV

May the Lord of peace himself give you peace at all times

in every way.

2 THESSALONIANS 3:16 ESV

If people's thinking is controlled by the sinful self, there

is death. But if their thinking is controlled by the Spirit,

there is life and peace.

ROMANS 8:6 NCV

I am Victorious

Thanks be to God! He gives us the victory
through our Lord Jesus Christ.

1 Corinthians 15:57 NIV

Can anything ever separate us from Christ's love?
Does it mean he no longer loves us if we have trouble
or calamity, or are persecuted, or hungry, or destitute,
or in danger, or threatened with death?
No, despite all these things, overwhelming victory is
ours through Christ, who loved us.

Romans 8:35, 37 NLT

Commit your actions to the LORD,
and your plans will succeed.

Proverbs 16:3 NLT

Thanks be to God, who always leads us in triumph
in Christ, and manifests through us the sweet aroma
of the knowledge of Him in every place.

2 Corinthians 2:14 nasb

In fact, this is love for God: to keep his commands.
And his commands are not burdensome, for everyone
born of God overcomes the world. This is the victory
that has overcome the world, even our faith. Who is it that
overcomes the world? Only the one who believes
that Jesus is the Son of God.

1 John 5:3-5 niv

Victory comes from you, O Lord.
May you bless your people.

Psalm 3:8 nlt

I am Whole

God made my life complete
when I placed all the pieces before him....
God rewrote the text of my life
when I opened the book of my heart to his eyes.

PSALM 18:20, 24 MSG

For you who fear my name, the sun of righteousness shall
rise with healing in its wings.

MALACHI 4:2 ESV

He will take our weak mortal bodies and change them
into glorious bodies like his own, using the same power
with which he will bring everything under his control.

PHILIPPIANS 3:21 NLT

What a God we have! And how fortunate we are to
have him, this Father of our Master Jesus! Because Jesus
was raised from the dead, we've been given a brand-new
life and have everything to live for, including a future in
heaven—and the future starts now! God is keeping careful
watch over us and the future. The Day is coming when
you'll have it all—life healed and whole.

1 Peter 1:3–5 MSG

This is how much God loved the world:
He gave his Son, his one and only Son.
And this is why: so that no one need be destroyed;
by believing in him, anyone can have
a whole and lasting life.

John 3:16 MSG